EARTHFORMS

By Martha London

Consultant: Beth Gambro
Reading Specialist, Yorkville, Illinois

Minneapolis, Minnesota

Teaching Tips

Before Reading

- Look at the cover of the book. Discuss the picture and the title.
- Ask readers to brainstorm a list of what they already know about caves. What can they expect to see in the book?
- Go on a picture walk, looking through the pictures to discuss vocabulary and make predictions about the text.

During Reading

- Read for purpose. Encourage readers to think about characteristics of caves.
- Ask readers to look for the details of the book. How do caves form?
- If readers encounter an unknown word, ask them to look at the sounds in the word. Then, ask them to look at the rest of the page. Are there any clues to help them understand?

After Reading

- Encourage readers to pick a buddy and reread the book together.
- Ask readers to name two things you might find in caves. Find the pages that tell about these things.
- Ask readers to write or draw something they learned about caves.

Credits
Cover and title page, © Pierrick Lemaret/iStock; 3, © OlyaSolodenko/iStock; 5, © Pictures-and-Pixels/iStock; 7, © earleliason/iStock; 8–9, © Fyletto/iStock; 10, © ES3N/iStock; 11, © fatido/iStock; 13, © alan64/iStock; 14–15, © brunovalenzano/Adobe Stock; 16–17, © Juhku/Adobe Stock; 18, © John Triumfante/Adobe Stock; 19, © Filip-Serban/iStock; 21, © Petro/Adobe Stock; 22T, © pingebat/Shutterstock; 22M, © kid315/Shutterstock; 22B, © Dave Bunnell/Creative Commons Attribution-Share Alike 4.0 International; 23TL, © Wirestock/iStock; 23TM, © NADIA GALLEGOS/iStock; 23TR, © Finn Hafemann/iStock; 23BL, © Aleksandr Grechanyuk/iStock; 23BM, © Cavan Images/iStock; 23BR, © Lauzla/iStock.

See BearportPublishing.com for our statement on Generative AI Usage.

Library of Congress Cataloging-in-Publication Data

Names: London, Martha, author.
Title: Caves / by Martha London.
Description: Bearcub books. | Minneapolis, Minnesota : Bearport Publishing Company, [2025] | Series: Earthforms | Includes bibliographical references and index.
Identifiers: LCCN 2024021064 (print) | LCCN 2024021065 (ebook) | ISBN 9798892326209 (library binding) | ISBN 9798892327008 (paperback) | ISBN 9798892326605 (ebook)
Subjects: LCSH: Caves--Juvenile literature.
Classification: LCC GB601.2 .L66 2025 (print) | LCC GB601.2 (ebook) | DDC 551.44/7--dc23/eng/20240509
LC record available at https://lccn.loc.gov/2024021064
LC ebook record available at https://lccn.loc.gov/2024021065

For more information, write to Bearport Publishing, 5357 Penn Avenue South, Minneapolis, MN 55419.

Contents

A Rocky Room

There is a huge hole in a rock.

Water drips down its walls.

Plop, plop, plop.

Caves are amazing!

Caves are openings big enough to walk into.

Some go down into the ground.

Others form in mountains.

There are even caves in icy **glaciers**.

Say glaciers like GLAY-shurz

Most caves are made of rock.

They may have long **tunnels**.

There can also be large open areas inside.

Streams flow in some rock caves.

Sea caves form along the ocean.

Caves can be made by **lava**, too.

This **melted** rock cools into long tubes.

A lava cave

Many caves need water to form.

Water breaks apart rock.

It carries tiny bits away.

After a long time, this makes a cave.

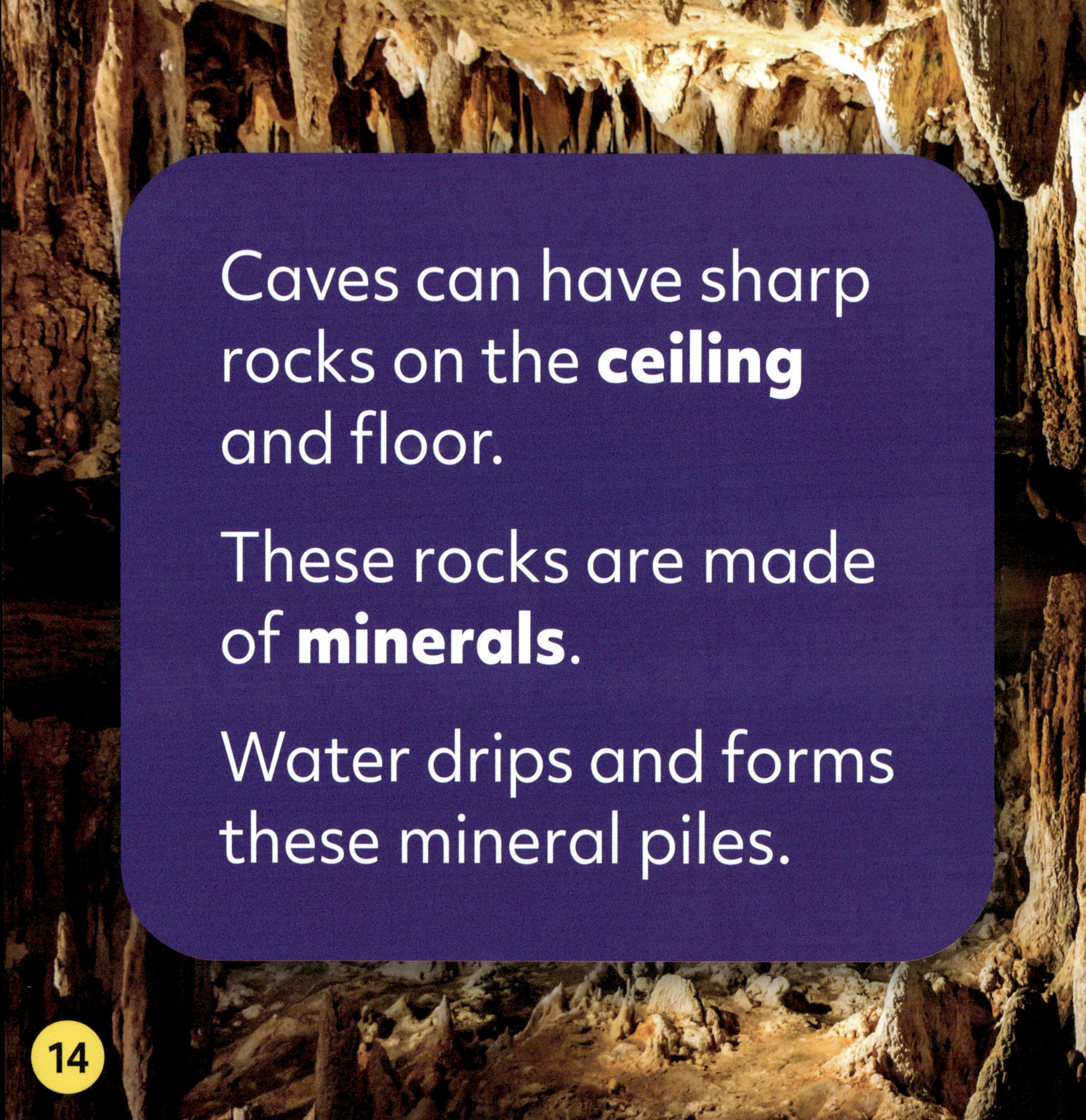

Caves can have sharp rocks on the **ceiling** and floor.

These rocks are made of **minerals**.

Water drips and forms these mineral piles.

Most caves are dark.

Light does not get far inside.

Caves do not heat up easily.

They are cool all year long.

Some animals live in caves.

They are used to the dark and cold.

Bats hang from the ceiling.

Bugs crawl all around.

There are many caves on Earth.

And new ones are always forming.

Grab your flashlight!

Let’s go find a cave.

Son Doong Cave

Son Doong is the largest cave on Earth.

Son Doong is in Vietnam.

Say Son Doong like *sun dong*. The name means mountain river cave.

This cave has its own forest. There are tall trees and many animals.

Glossary

ceiling the overhead inside of a room or space

glaciers huge pieces of ice

lava hot liquid rock that comes from a crack in the ground

melted changed from a solid to a liquid because of heat

minerals solid objects found in nature that are not plants or animals

tunnels passages under the ground

Index

Read More

Amstutz, Lisa J. *Caves (Earth's Landforms).* North Mankato, MN: Capstone Press, 2021.

Billings, Tanner. *Caves (Our Exciting Earth!).* New York: Gareth Stevens Publishing, 2023.

Learn More Online

1. Go to **FactSurfer.com** or scan the QR code below.
2. Enter "**Earthforms Caves**" into the search box.
3. Click on the cover of this book to see a list of websites.

About the Author

Martha London lives in Minnesota. She loves spending time outside.